SEE HOW THEY GROW
CHICK

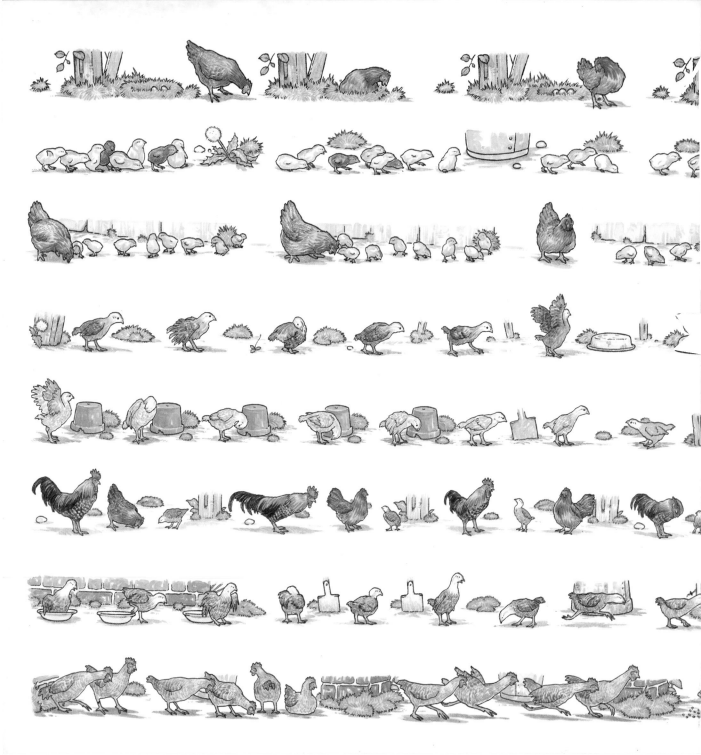

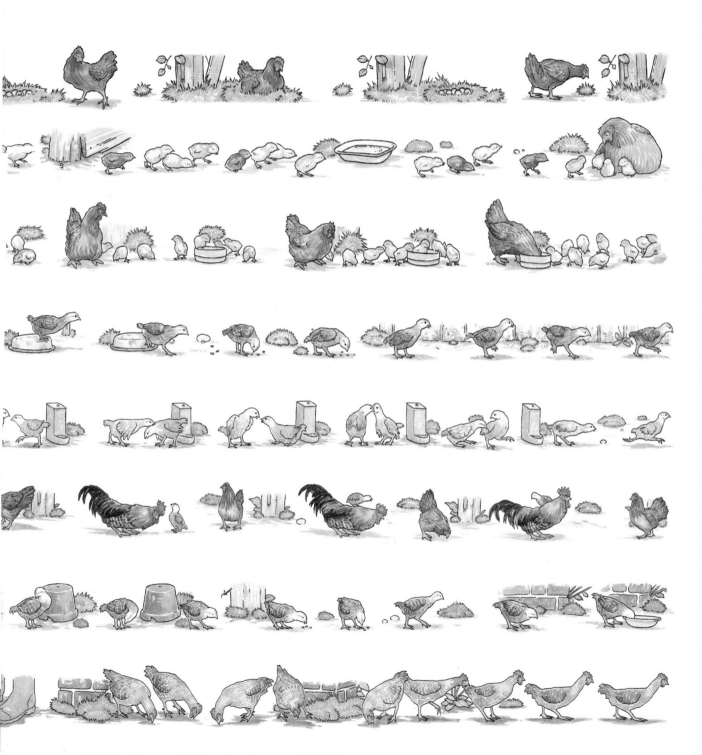

A DORLING KINDERSLEY BOOK

Written and edited by Angela Royston
Editor Mary Ling
Art Editor Nigel Hazle
Production Marguerite Fenn
Illustrators Rowan Clifford

Published in Great Britain by
Dorling Kindersley Limited
9 Henrietta Street, London WC2E 8PS

Paperback edition
2 4 6 8 10 9 7 5 3 1

Visit us on the World Wide Web at
http://:www.dk.com

A CIP catalogue record for this book is available
from the British Library

ISBN 0-7513-6628-5

Colour reproduction by Colourscan, Singapore
Printed in Singapore by Imago

SEE HOW THEY GROW
CHICK

photographed by
JANE BURTON

DORLING KINDERSLEY
London • New York • Moscow • Sydney

Hatching

This is my mother. She is sitting on her eggs. Inside each egg a chick is growing. One of them is me.

I start to chip around the inside of my egg shell.

I push my shell apart.

At last I am free.

Out of the egg

I am one hour old. My brothers
and sisters have
hatched too.
We are
chirping to
each other.

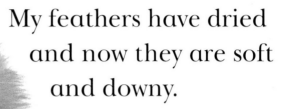

My feathers have dried
and now they are soft
and downy.

Learning to feed

I am three days old and I am feeling
hungry. My mother is eating seed.
How does she do it?
I watch her
carefully.

I stretch
up and take the seed
from her beak.

It tastes so good
I decide to peck
some myself.

A drink of water

I am eight days old now. New feathers are growing on my wings.

What is Mum doing? She is dipping her beak into a bowl of water.

I hop into the bowl.
The water is cool and wet.
My sister is getting in too.

False alarm

I am two weeks old.
Today I am looking
for food with
my mother.

Is something wrong?
My mother is flapping
her wings.
She clucks
at us to run
away.

It is a false alarm.
Nothing is wrong.
Mother calls us
back.

Meeting Dad

I am four weeks old now. I am growing bigger every day.

Here is my father.
Look how big he is!

Dad is very friendly.
He lets me ride on
his back.

Growing bigger

I am eight weeks old and
all my feathers have
grown.

I have a
bright red
comb on
my head and a
red wattle under my beak.

I am big and strong. At last I can look after myself.

I use my beak to keep myself clean and tidy. I am proud of my fine feathers.

See how I grew

The egg

One hour old

Three days old

Eight days old

Two weeks old

Four weeks old   Eight weeks old

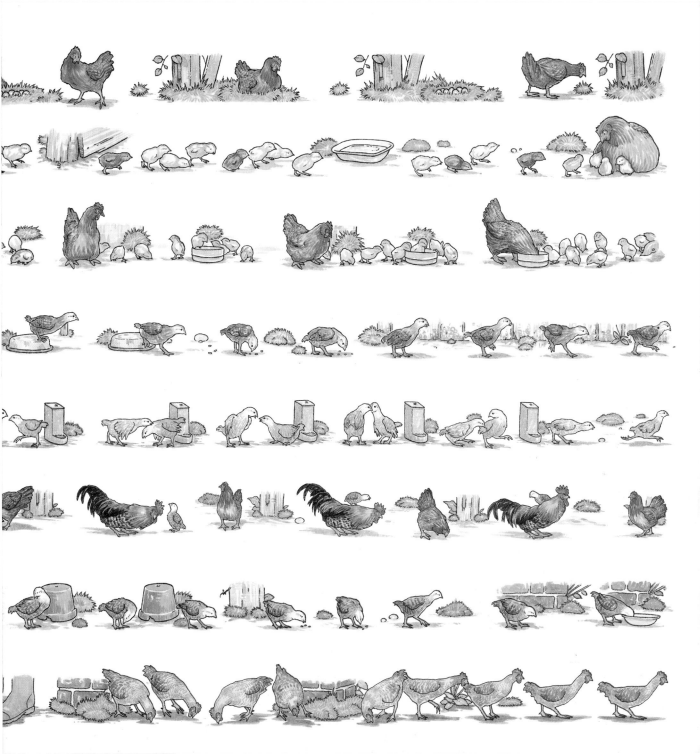